BOAS AND OTHER NON-VENOMOUS SNAKES
KW-002

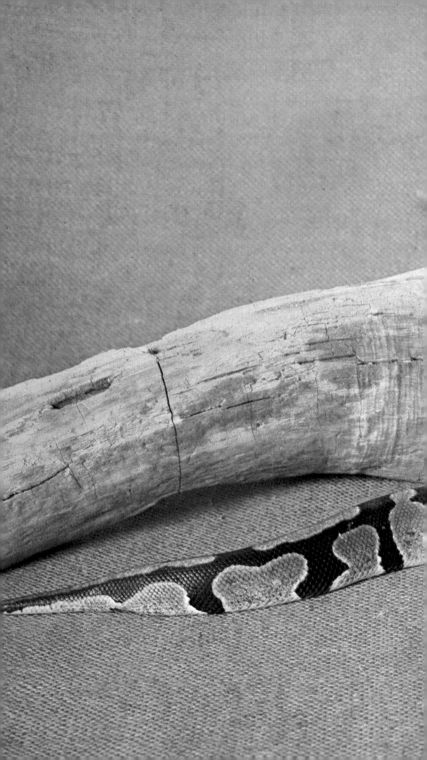

Contents

Photographers: W.R. Branch, Dr. Warren Burgess, Courtesy of Chester Zoo, Courtesy of Cotswold Wildlife Park, Guido Dingerkus, John Dommers, W. Frank, Isabelle Francais, M. Freiberg, Jeff Gee, R. Hansen, R.T. Hoser, Ray Hunziker, B. Kahl, John T. Kellnhauser, Alex Kerstitch, S. Kochetov, R. Koenig, H. Kratzer, Courtesy of R.E. Kunte, Courtesy of London Zoo, Ken Lucas, J. Maier, G. Marcuse, S. Minton, Louis Porras, K. Progscha, P.J. Stafford, J.P. Swaak, E. Zimmermann.

Overleaf: The ball python of western Africa, Python regius, *is attractive but difficult to keep in captivity.* **Title page:** *An attractive boa constrictor.*

Originally published in German by Franckh'sche Verlagshandlung, W. Keller and Company, Stuttgart 1978, under the title *Schlangen im Terrarium: Haltung und Pflege ungifter Schlangen.* First edition ® 1978 by Franckh'sche Verlagshandlung. Copyright 1979 by T.F.H. Publications, Inc. Ltd. for English translation. A considerable amount of additional new material has been added to the literal German-English translation, including but not limited to additional photographs. Copyright is also claimed for this new material.

Distributed in the UNITED STATES by T.F.H. Publications, Inc., One T.F.H. Plaza, Neptune City, NJ 07753; in CANADA to the Pet Trade by H & L Pet Supplies Inc., 27 Kingston Crescent, Kitchener, Ontario N2B 2T6; Rolf C. Hagen Ltd., 3225 Sartelon Street, Montreal 382 Quebec; in CANADA to the Book Trade by Macmillan of Canada (A Division of Canada Publishing Corporation), 164 Commander Boulevard, Agincourt, Ontario M1S 3C7; in ENGLAND by T.F.H. Publications Limited, Cliveden House/Priors Way/Bray, Maidenhead, Berkshire SL6 2HP, England; in AUSTRALIA AND THE SOUTH PACIFIC by T.F.H. (Australia) Pty. Ltd., Box 149, Brookvale 2100 N.S.W., Australia; in NEW ZEALAND by Ross Haines & Son, Ltd., 82 D Elizabeth Knox Place, Panmure, Auckland, New Zealand; in the PHILIPPINES by Bio-Research, 5 Lippay Street, San Lorenzo Village, Makati Rizal; in SOUTH AFRICA by Multipet Pty. Ltd., Box 235 New Germany, South Africa 3620. Published by T.F.H. Publications, Inc. Manufactured in the United States of America by T.F.H. Publications, Inc.

BOAS
AND OTHER
NON-VENOMOUS
SNAKES

PROFESSOR DOCTOR WERNER FRANK
Translated by U. Erich Friese

A dice or tessellated snake, Natrix tesselata. This snake is more conspicuously marked than most water snakes.

Above: *A young emerald tree boa, Corallus caninus. Although adults are bright green, juveniles and subadults are various shades of orange. This species is rather difficult to acclimate.* **Below:** *A mussurana, Clelia clelia, devouring another snake. This large South American species feeds almost exclusively on snakes.*

Acknowledgment

I would like to express my thanks and gratitude to Mr. Henri Kratzer, Zurich (Switzerland), an experienced snake keeper, for the many interesting conversations I had with him, for reviewing this manuscript and for his constructive criticism.

Foreword

This book is not intended for those who believe that all snakes are not only venomous, but also attack, immediately and unprovoked, anyone who approaches them in the wild. Also, it was not written with those people in mind who consider snakes to be detestable, slimy creatures, and which therefore have to be totally avoided. Instead, this book is meant for those who have a natural affinity for all animals, including reptiles, and especially for snakes. It is intended to be a preliminary guide to the snakes which can be kept satisfactorily in captivity and to distinguish them from those which are unsuitable.

I am fully aware that within the limited space available not all species can be dealt with in depth. Yet, I believe that I can provide to the hobbyist sufficient useful information to help him in his efforts to keep snakes satisfactorily in captivity. In addition, what is going to be said here might also save many snakes which are often condemned to vegetate under totally unsatisfactory conditions and under inadequate care. Usually these unfortunate animals are only relieved from their misery by death, and then, as a rule, they only make room for another quickly acquired death candidate.

Below: Headstudy of a northern water snake, Nerodia sipedon. ***Opposite:*** *A Mandarin rat snake,* Elaphe mandarina.

Lampropeltis zonata, *one of the attractive western American coral kingsnakes.*

Above: Boa constrictor, *the most commonly kept boa, in a well-planted cage.* **Below:** *The rainbow boa,* Epicrates cenchria. *Note the highly iridescent coloration that gives this snake its name. The conspicuous spots indicate that this specimen is a subadult.*

Snakes at Home?

Yes, but only when the necessary conditions are available. One important prerequisite is that snake-keeping in an apartment or home is accepted by all concerned. If snakes are rejected in principle by someone in the home, and if accommodation of snakes in a separate room is not possible, one is best advised to look for some other animal to keep. Another important point to keep in mind is the cage in which the snakes are to be kept; that is, its position and decoration. For instance, it would hardly make sense to set up an aqua-terrarium and to acquire burrowing desert snakes for it.

It is equally important to be assured of a regular food supply before the snakes are acquired. Therefore, one should know beforehand where the food animals can be obtained or whether these have to be bred by the hobbyist in his own food animal breeding facilities. Since the latter option usually involves rats and mice, this can conceivably meet considerable opposition from other people in the apartment or home concerned.

Below: A rat snake, Elaphe obsoleta quadrivittata. *Races of* Elaphe obsoleta *are commonly found in farm areas.* **Opposite:** *A kingsnake,* Lampropeltis mexicana.

Above: The small flattened head and cylindrical body covered with small scales show that the Indian sand boa, *Eryx johnii,* is a burrowing species. *Below:* The Madagascar tree boa, *Sanzinia madagascariensis,* with its brown pattern against a gray background, is one of the most distinctively marked giant snakes.

Above: *The attractive reticulated python,* Python reticulatus, *is commonly kept but grows to an enormous size.* **Below:** *The dark or common subspecies of the Indian python,* Python molurus bivittatus.

Why Keep Snakes?

Pure sensationalism is a highly undesirable motive for keeping any animal. In this context, at least, the keeping of snakes is to be totally rejected. Apart from such superficial motives, there are a number of very legitimate reasons why snakes can be kept in captivity. These mainly include observation of the behavior of snakes, such as their feeding, mating and the possible rearing of young born in captivity. An important aspect of all reptile husbandry is the maintenance of accurate written records which can be used to reveal any irregularities in the food and feeding pattern, the shedding of skin or other abnormal behavior.

Many highly interesting scientific facts have been ascertained this way by observant hobbyists. Such studies can be made not only on rare and expensive snakes, but also on those which are common and easily available and are not threatened by extinction. Therefore, the beginning hobbyist must not let himself be persuaded by an unscrupulous dealer to purchase a snake which he cannot keep satisfactorily. This way the hobbyist can contribute significantly to the survival of snakes which have become rare or those which cannot be kept in captivity. A reduced demand will cause the importation of endangered species to decline and hopefully to cease completely.

Apart from domestic laws in different countries governing the purchase and sale of all protected animals, there is also the *Washington Agreement for the Protection of Endangered Species*, which has come into force recently. This agreement covers endangered animal and plant species, and specifically lists a number of snakes. The responsible reptile hobbyist should use the following list as a firm guide in his decision about which species to purchase.

APPENDIX I

Exportation of animals, listed in Appendix I, is only permitted if an export license, granted by the relevant department of the exporting country, is on hand. An export license can only be granted if an import license from the importing country is available. Such licenses are only issued when the conditions, mentioned in the Agreement relevant to the acquisition, transport, etc., have been met, and the exporting country has ascertained that the export is not detrimental to the survival of the species. The most important point in considering requests for such permit is—apart from an examination of the proposed accommodation and

Opposite: A newborn Cook's tree boa, Corallus enydris cookii. This is a subspecies of the garden tree boa.

husbandry facilities—that such permit cannot be issued if the importation is mainly for commercial purposes.

Family Boidae (Giant Snakes)
Light Indian Python, *Python molurus molurus*
Puerto Rico Boa, *Epicrates inornatus inornatus*
Jamaica Boa, *Epicrates subflavus*
Madagascar Boa, *Acrantophis madagascariensis*
Madagascar Tree Boa, *Sanzinia madagascariensis*
Round Island Boas, *Bolyerei multicarinata, Casarea dussumieri.*

A pair of Cuban boas, *Epicrates angulifer. Members of this species often dwell in caves and eat bats.*

APPENDIX II

The exportation of species listed in Appendix II requires an export permit, which is issued under the same criteria indicated for Appendix I. The importation of specimens of a species listed in Appendix II requires the presentation of an official export permit from the country of origin. In the event of a trans-shipment (re-sale) an export permit, issued by the country into which the animal was previously imported, is also required.

Family Boidae (Giant Snakes)

Since 1977, all species, as far as these are not already listed in Appendix I.

Family Colubridae (Colubrid snakes)

Brazilian Smooth Snake, *Cyclagras gigas*

Mussurana, *Clelia clelia*

Indian Egg-eating Snake, *Elachistodon westermanni*

Mountain Garter Snake, *Thamnophis elegans hammondi.*

A captive-bred amelanic (albino) corn snake, Elaphe guttata. *Note the red eyes on this specimen.*

Accommodations

Although a wide selection of glass aquarium tanks is available, only a few suitable snake cage models (terrariums or vivariums, as reptile cages are commonly called) are available commercially. In view of the scarcity of suitable snake cages, hobbyists are best advised to construct their own. This way special requirements, particularly for certain species, can be met right from the start.

It is important that the cage is not too small, because snakes must have ample room to move about. In planning the cage, consideration has to be given to the ecological requirements of the animals. Therefore, the hobbyist has to be certain whether a special cage, possibly with a container large enough for bathing, has to be constructed or whether he can get by with a small water dish for drinking. Also of paramount importance are adequate heating provisions. These include substrate or radiant heaters, which should be controlled by a thermostat. Lighting should also be regulated by a time switch. The cage must not be too tightly sealed, as this would inhibit adequate ventilation. Conceivably, several cages of variable sizes can be constructed as a single unit with removable partitions.

It is important for the health of snakes to shed their old skin, or molt periodically. The animals can only do this satisfactorily when some rough surfaces are available in the cages. Ideal are branches, rocks, etc., which cut the old skin around the lips and which help to strip off the old skin while the snake winds around and about rough surfaces. Many snake species also require branches for climbing. Placing suitable plants into a snake cage is not only an exercise in esthetics; in fact, it is required for green snakes and for those species which require a high humidity (lush plant growth increases the humidity).

The substrate is determined largely by the ecological requirements of the species to be kept. Smooth gravel (never use rough quartz sand) is, for instance, ideal for giant snakes. Burrowing boas should be provided with adequate sand, and burrowing pipe snakes prefer moist humus soil. Loose top soil or, better yet, peat covered with live moss is suitable for garter snakes.

Decay, often encountered with the prevailing conditions in a wet terrarium, can be prevented by meticulous cleanliness and frequent changes of the substrate. However, even a cage without elaborate decoration can produce excellent husbandry results.

Opposite: A rat snake, Elaphe obsoleta rossalleni. *Snake cages may contain furnishings such as rocks and branches which will add interest to the cage as well as providing hiding places for the inhabitants.*

The *Agkistrodon*, bred commercially in a European snake farm, is a good example. These snakes are bred continuously in cages, located in a temperature-controlled room, which contain only a bathing dish and a piece of corrugated cardboard as substrate. The cardboard is replaced every time the animals have defecated, so that absolutely hygienic conditions exist at all times.

Cleanliness, which is important in the husbandry of all animals, is equally necessary for snakes. The drinking water should be replaced daily and the water in the bathing

An African rock python, Python sebae natalensis. *This species is found throughout southern Africa.*

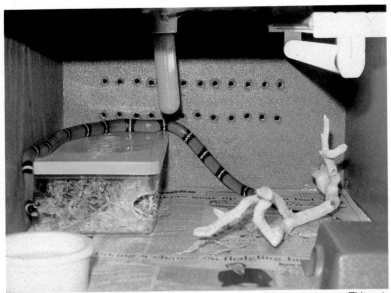

A sinaloau milk snake, Lampropeltis triangulum sinaloau, *in a typical cage. This set-up contains a branch, heating bulbs, a box of moist moss, and, of course, a water dish.*

container at the latest when it has become soiled with feces or other debris. Feces, as well as pieces of shed skin, etc., lying around the cage, have to be removed frequently. The entire substrate, possibly including the rocks and climbing branches, should be replaced at frequent intervals. Unfortunately, germs, bacteria and fungi, as well as insects (springtails, etc.) and mites accumulate in the substrate. These are then destroyed by removing the substrate and thoroughly cleaning the cage.

If several cages are maintained, each one should be serviced with separate cleaning equipment, feeding utensils, etc., thus avoiding the transfer of harmful organisms from one cage into the others. Furthermore, it is advisable that all equipment be sterilized in boiling water or in a disinfecting solution after each use. It is, of course, equally important that the hands are properly disinfected after snakes from different cages have been handled and after all daily maintenance work on the cages has been completed.

Quarantine and Snake Hygiene

A hobbyist just starting out has, of course, no quarantine problems with the initial lot of animals. However, any subsequent additions will have to be placed into quarantine for several weeks (the longer the better) and kept totally isolated from all other snakes in a separate room.

Quarantine cages must be set up so that they are virtually sterile, containing only the bare essentials. These should include a cage bottom made of materials which can be easily cleaned. Slate tiles, for instance, covered with old newspapers can be changed quickly and easily. Also included should be a climbing branch with smooth bark or stem, a rough-surfaced rock for assisting the snakes in shedding their skin and a drinking dish (for some species also a large bathing container).

Optimum temperature conditions must also be provided, possibly through built-in heating coils. Regular, thorough disinfection of all accessory handling and feeding equipment is also of paramount importance.

Before a snake is placed into

Below: A milk snake in a cage utilizing gravel for the cage bottom. Gravel is not a good medium for the bottom of a quarantine cage, as it is difficult to keep clean. It is fine, however, for an everyday cage. Opposite: A corn snake, Elaphe guttata.

the cage, it should be bathed in water of approximately 30°C in order to remove any attached dirt particles. This process also makes it easier for the snake to get rid of hardened pieces of feces and solid uric acid particles from the cloaca. Such a bath also facilitates the absorption of water through the skin.

Since most snakes do not willingly stay in such a bath, their escape has to be prevented by a lid, which must, however, permit adequate ventilation of the bathing container. A rough-surfaced rock or large stone in the bath gives the snake adequate support. Only

after this procedure has been satisfactorily completed should the snake be transferred to the quarantine cage.

While the animal is being handled, it should be thoroughly inspected for any external injuries as well as for ectoparasites such as ticks and mites. Similarly, the feces must be checked for parasites and their eggs or larvae. Nematodes and tapeworm segments can often be recognized with the naked eye, but a microscopic examination for worm eggs and encysted protozoans (resting stage of single-celled organisms) is usually more

A subspecies of the rainbow boa, Epicrates cenchria crassus. Epicrates *species are usually found close to water; therefore, the air in their surroundings should not be too dry.*

A dice snake. Snakes of the genus Natrix *are called water or grass snakes, and they are generally considered to be easy to tame.*

thorough and successful.

If the feces is of a mushy, rather smelly consistency and of grayish coloration, or if the animal either refuses food or regurgitates partially digested, rather odorous food animals after a few days, this is in most cases indicative of acute gastroenteritis, an infection of the digestive tract. The feces of those snakes which feed on small mammals (rats, mice) are firm, are excreted sausage-like and have a brown-red to black coloration. Usually they contain a lot of hair from the food animals. When newly hatched chicks are fed the feces have a somewhat softer, almost mushy consistency; however, the food in healthy specimens is never regurgitated. When feeding snakes fish, the feces are similarly soft and smell equally bad. The behavior of newly acquired snakes should be closely watched for some time to check their interest—or lack of it—in food animals, shedding their skin and defecation. Beyond that, there is generally very little the hobbyist can do.

It is important that the feces, as well as the rock-hard pieces of uric acid, which are excreted by the kidneys and which are insoluble in water, be removed regularly from the cage. Although there are some parasites which affect the urinary tract and whose eggs are found only in these solids, the treatment of these is impossible. It is, therefore, pointless to examine these pieces of uric acid.

Feeding Snakes

With some exceptions, usually arising from conditioning in captivity, snakes feed only on live prey. For their normal digestive process it is important that live food, together with an optimum temperature, be provided. These factors are often not considered sufficiently by hobbyists. A healthy specimen may well take food even in colder surroundings, but invariably the food animals will be regurgitated—barely macerated—within a few days, since digestion simply cannot take place. Such problems can easily be solved by increasing the temperature.

A well-acclimated snake will always accept its proper food and digest it completely within a few days, so that feces can be expected to be excreted after eight to ten days. If a snake has not taken any food for some time, excretion will take longer. The convoluted digestive tract is completely empty and the passage of food takes correspondingly longer.

When keeping snakes, one always has to remember that different animals—even those of the same species—may have different food and feeding preferences which have to be catered to. It is also known that some snakes suddenly and for no apparent reason refuse their usual type of food and will starve until a new suitable food is eventually found and accepted. For instance, an anaconda, *Eunectes murinus*,

about 1.2m long, which had been kept temporarily in a zoo terrarium and had there taken fish as food, refused all food for weeks on end, although mice, rats, hamsters and guinea pigs were also offered. Then, one day when newly hatched chickens were available, the snake took eight of these within less than half an hour.

Generally, it can be said that any snake which is healthy and is kept under optimum conditions will, after an acclimating period, readily accept food when the right type of prey is offered.

Unfortunately, current knowledge about the food requirements of some species is still somewhat limited, and more first-hand experiences and

Opposite: A rat snake. The majority of Elaphe *species feed on small mammals such as mice and rats.*

...servations are needed. So, for instance, to this day it has rarely been possible to get the highly venomous sea snakes (Hydrophiidae) or wart (file) snakes (Acrochordidae), which also live in water, or for that matter the tentacled snake (*Erpeton*), to accept food regularly over prolonged periods. The burrowing Uropeltidae and the blind snakes, Typhlopidae and Leptotyphlopidae, only very rarely can be persuaded to take food in

FEEDING SNAKES

captivity. If food is taken, it is usually of a type which is nutritionally unsatisfactory, so the animals die sooner or later. If, however, proper environmental and ecological conditions are provided, even difficult snakes will readily accept food. This writer has kept two pipe snakes, *Cylindrophis*, for about ten years without any problems, during which time they took, apart from fish, the occasional lizard or gecko.

Force-feeding is only called for when an animal has become very weak, so that it does not have the strength to feed on its own, or when newly born snakes are to be raised. The problems in force-feeding small snakes often arise from the non-availability of suitably small food items. In addition, it is often not taken into consideration that the food requirements change significantly from juvenile to adult animals.

If force-feeding cannot be avoided, there are several ways to accomplish this. One is by giving different sizes of fish with slender bodies. Because of the fish's structure and slimy skin, they will easily slide inside the digestive tract of the snakes. Small strips of lean (muscle) meat can also be used when nothing else is available. In any event, food items used in this manner can be supplemented with a sprinkling of vitamins or preferably with an injection into the food of an aqueous vitamin combination. The food has to be massaged slowly

A tropical rat snake, Spilotes pullatus mexicanus. *Tropical rat snakes grow very large, and they feed on birds and small mammals.*

A California kingsnake, Lampropeltis getulus californiae. *Kingsnakes are known for feeding on other snakes, and* Lampropeltis getulus *is known by many as a venomous snake eater.*

down the esophagus and into the stomach.

Another method is an American technique which is often used in snake farms. American literature also recommends this technique for use by hobbyists. This involves the mixing of various food items, which, after the addition of vitamins, minerals and trace elements, are then macerated and liquefied in a blender. Such a mixture is then further diluted with water or sometimes with blood, so that it is of a consistency which can be forced through a plastic or rubber tube with a large syringe as far as possible down the esophagus, or ideally directly into the stomach. I personally reject this method categorically, since in my opinion it counteracts the normal physiological process, so that digestion together with the peristalsis of the digestive tract is not fully functional because of the absence of required roughage materials. On the other hand, this method is, of course, quite acceptable when it is used to feed an extremely weak snake in order to bring it back into proper condition or when diseased animals have to be orally medicated.

Regrettably, some so-called hobbyists are too set in their ways to accept well meant advice for the benefit of their animals. I recall the case of a hobbyist whose sick snake we treated. I offered some advice in regard to the feeding of his snake. This he abruptly rejected, with remarks that if I was of the opinion that a boa or python requires rats, guinea pigs or rabbits as food, I must be rather inexperienced. In the future he would rather treat his animals himself, since it was a well-known fact that the best method was to force-feed his snakes with strips of veal or beef, as he had been doing for many years. It is difficult to deal with such ingrained attitudes, and all efforts would no doubt have been in vain.

It is generally true that snakes, in comparison to all other reptiles, have the most irregular food urge. As a rule they should only be fed every ten to 14 days. This interval can be extended by another one or two weeks during the period when the snake is shedding its skin. Snakes which feed on fish and earthworms have a higher metabolic rate than those utilizing birds or small mammals as food. However, a regularly feeding snake has a tendency to become too fat rather than too undernourished.

Young snakes sometimes take food as often as it is offered, which of course leads to fairly rapid growth. Therefore, growth can be influenced, within certain limits, through a strictly controlled diet, without actually starving the snake. It is even possible to forego feeding for the duration of a three-week holiday, as long as ample drinking and, if needed, bathing water is provided. The extremes are found in the giant snakes, which sometimes, and for inexplicable reasons, will not accept food for several months. The extraordinary phenomenon is that the animals rarely ever lose weight during these periods of starvation. It is reported, for instance, that a large python once refused food for 49 months before it started to feed again! Such hunger periods can, of course, only be endured without detrimental effects by snakes which are in good condition.

It has been observed that hunger periods of several weeks in duration are part of the normal life cycle in some species. For instance, the females of the Old World pythons will not take food during the approximately eight to ten weeks they are incubating

Kingsnakes are difficult to feed, as smaller snakes for their consumption are not easy to obtain.

their eggs. Cessation of feeding may sometimes start before the eggs are laid. This then appears to be a biological regulating mechanism which prevents the developing eggs, before they are actually laid, from being damaged during strangling and swallowing of prey. It usually takes three to four months from copulation to the eggs being laid.

The species diversity of snakes is matched by a variety of different food and feeding requirements. These range from snakes which have highly specific requirements to those which will accept a wide variety of food items. Most suitable for a life in captivity are, of course, snakes which will feed on a variety of prey instead of those which insist on a specific type of food. Snakes which feed on bird eggs in the wild, such as the African egg-eating snake, *Dasypeltis scabra*, or those which feed on termites or other burrowing, soft-skinned invertebrates, are hard to keep. The tropical blind snakes, Typhlopidae and Leptotyphlopidae, fall into these latter food categories. It is therefore self-explanatory that, for instance, the snail-eating snakes (*Dipsas*), with their short skulls and extended lower jaws which are adapted to pull snails from their shells, cannot accept any substitute foods.

Snake-keeping is best confined to those species which feed readily on rats and mice, food items which can easily be provided. Such a diet can be supplemented and enlarged with guinea pigs, rabbits, chickens and ducks (for particularly large specimens of giant snakes), which are all commercially available. Those hobbyists who intend to pursue snake-keeping in earnest

A four-lined rat snake, Elaphe quatuorlineata. *Snakes of this species sometimes feed on birds and their eggs.*

A red rat snake, Elaphe guttata guttata. *The prey of rat snakes is killed by constriction; therefore, it is recommended that food animals be killed before being fed to the snake only if that snake is known to be an inept constrictor and that death for these animals would prevent suffering.*

will, sooner or later, be compelled to start up their own animal breeding facility to provide adequate food for their snakes. This is best done in a room removed from the main living quarters, because the bad smell from such a facility can be a serious problem. White mice, which are most commonly bred at home, emit a rather penetrating odor not acceptable to too many people living in an apartment or house. Since this characteristic smell is caused by natural excretion, regular cleaning has little effect upon it. Odorless rodents such as gerbils or sand rats are more difficult to breed and the young in each litter are fewer. Moreover, these animals are cute, so that in any family which is fond of animals there would be immediate trauma when these rodents are to be fed to the snakes.

Proper husbandry methods are also very important when breeding animals as snake food, and cleanliness is absolutely vital. As far as the food for these animals is concerned, the days are over when uneaten leftovers such as old bread, boiled potatoes and occasionally some cereal and a little milk were considered to be sufficient. Even animals intended only as food for snakes have specific nutritional requirements which can only be met by standardized diets. That they must also be kept under strictly hygienic conditions and in suitable cages need not be stressed further. Only healthy food animals which have been raised under proper nutritional conditions will provide adequate nutrition for snakes. With such an adequate supply of self-bred food animals on hand,

FEEDING SNAKES

only newly acquired snakes in poor condition and sick snakes will then require additional vitamin and mineral supplements. Should this become necessary, the required multi-vitamin mixture can be injected into the food animals in an aqueous solution before they are offered to the snakes.

Newly hatched chicks, which are usually available throughout the year from major hatcheries, are also a good and inexpensive (cocks are sold very cheaply) food for snakes.

When fish-eating snakes are kept, things become a bit more difficult, but most fishermen know where small bait fish can be purchased at little expense. When baby snakes of such species have to be fed with the proper (small) food, contact with a tropical fish hobbyist is often useful. Their excess of newly bred tropical fish, such as guppies and others, can often be obtained without difficulties and at low cost.

Somewhat more difficult to keep are snakes which feed on amphibians, as these are often only available seasonally. The

The European grass snake, Natrix natrix, *feeds on frogs. Some subspecies may feed on lizards and mice.*

A pair of Asiatic rock pythons, also known as black-tailed pythons, Python molurus molurus. *Most pythons feed on mammals and birds.*

same problem occurs with lizard-eating snakes. Before purchasing such species, be sure you will be able to have enough food on hand all year around. In many countries the problem is compounded because amphibians and lizards are protected by law.

On the other hand, snakes which feed on invertebrates such as earthworms or crickets and grasshoppers are somewhat easier to keep. Garter snakes, *Thamnophis*, will always—except during the winter months—have a sufficient earthworm supply from a crate filled with earth and stocked with an adequate supply of worms. Incidentally, earthworms should not be collected off asphalt road surfaces because of an acute danger of poisoning the snakes. Breeding or purchasing crickets, etc., rarely presents any problems.

Some important remarks should be added to the topic of food and feeding at this stage. Hands which have handled rats and mice must be thoroughly washed before the hobbyist can safely reach into the snake cage. The sense of smell in a snake is far better developed than its visual acuity, so it is easy for the animal to mistake the hand for prey, something which can indeed be unpleasant. One should only offer as many food animals as are immediately eaten. Those not eaten should be removed at night because they might gnaw on the snakes. In case they cannot be caught, baited traps have to be placed in the snake cage; at the very least put in some mouse food in the form of dry pellets.

If several snakes are kept together in the same cage, feeding has to be closely watched, since it is easy for two snakes to grab the same food animal and it becomes possible for one snake to swallow the other. Young snakes, because of their aggressive feeding behavior, are particularly prone to such accidents; therefore, it is important to be watchful. Nevertheless, should such a feeding accident happen, the entwined snakes should be dumped into cold water or smoke can be blown into their partially opened mouths.

An albino red rat snake. The appetite of snakes is very variable. Some individuals may go for months without feeding, while others require a meal every ten to 14 days.

An eastern kingsnake, Lampropeltis getulus holbrooki. *Cleanliness is imperative for keeping healthy snakes. Therefore, all uneaten food should be removed from the cage immediately.*

Alternatively, a cotton ball drenched with ether, ammonia or some other strong smelling fluid, held in front of the mouths of the animals, will usually cause them to let go of their prey and of each other.

Once food animals have been in a snake cage, they should not be used again. The danger of transferring harmful organisms such as bacteria, encysted protozoans (amoebas), worm eggs, mites and ticks is quite acute. Therefore, the apparently wasteful and expensive practice of disposing of uneaten food is in the long run the better procedure and ultimately the least expensive way, because the snakes remain healthy and stay alive.

Morphology and Ecology of Snakes

A snake is conspicuous through its elongated body, which is covered by scales. It does not have any appendages. Snakes are distinguished from legless lizards by the presence of large ventral scales covering the entire width of the body. Those horny scales come in different sizes and colors which form patterns with distinct species characteristics. Over each eye is a colorless, arched scale, forming the spectacles.

The snake has to shed its skin at regular intervals, a process which is under the controlling influence of hormones. It is initiated eight to ten days before the skin is actually shed, and during this period snakes are nearly blind. Usually they will not accept any food and will remain hidden out of sight or spend their time lying in the water bath if one is provided. Here it must be said that the cornified layer of the epidermis is being formed continually by the underlying layer (stratum germinativum) of the epidermis so the outer layers (stratum spinosum, stratum granulosum, stratum lucidum and the completely horny stratum corneum), which are the thicker portions of the epidermis, are replaced by those developing underneath. As the underlying

An albino California kingsnake of the striped phase. The skin of a snake is at its brightest after an old layer has just been shed.

A red milk snake, Lampropeltis triangulum syspila. *Just prior to shedding its skin, the snake's eyes will become cloudy.*

layers develop, nerve and circulatory connections with the outermost layer are lost and there is a general loosening between the outer layers. This is accomplished through the diffusion of lymph between the old and new layers and through the pressure exerted by minute rugosities in the new layer. Shedding of the outer layer is generally initiated at the head region. A swelling mechanism causes an enlargement of the head through an abrupt increase in the blood pressure in the veins of the head. In most snakes the sloughed layer comes off intact.

It is important that the skin shedding process is completed successfully. In the event of complications, a snake can be immersed in lukewarm water to make it easier for the animal to get rid of its old skin. Any remaining pieces of old skin can give a foothold to fungal diseases. The area of the spectacles, if this section is not shed, is particularly susceptible. Invariably this will cause an infection between the pieces of the old skin and the new

The cleared and stained skeleton of the common water snake, Nerodia sipedon.

A diamond python, Morelia spilotes spilotes. *Members of the genus* Morelia *are now often classified under the genus* Python. *These snakes are considered difficult to keep.*

layer underneath, which can lead to permanent blindness or death through blood poisoning.

Remnants of appendages are only found in some of the more primitive snakes, such as the Boidae (giant snakes), but these vestigial legs serve no functional purpose. The distal parts of hind appendages are externally visible as horny protrusions (claws). In fact, the length of these can be used to distinguish males from females.

The basic, elongated snake body shows many special morphological adaptations to the ecologically prevailing conditions encountered by various species. There are snakes with an extremely thin, elongated tail, such as the long-nosed whip snake, *Ahatulla nasuta*, or the tree-dwelling green snakes, *Leptophis* spp.. Others have a short and blunt tail, such as the Uropeltidae, or snakes with a stumpy tail, as seen in the pipe snakes, Aniliidae. There are also snakes with a rather plumpish body, such as the blood python, *Python curtus*. The laterally compressed tail of the sea snakes, Hydrophiidae, is a rather special adaptation for swimming. A similar specialization can be seen in the blind or worm snakes, Typhlopidae and Leptotyphlopidae, with their rounded-off tail. In fact, in these snakes the blunt head, which is used for burrowing, can only be distinguished from the tail by the presence of tiny black eyes.

The different body shapes of snakes are well reflected in their skeletal structures, particularly in the bones of the head. Thus, one can distinguish not only the burrowing snakes from those which remain above ground, but also differences between venomous and non-venomous species. Non-venomous snakes

A fish snake, Natrix piscator. *This species is often classified in the genus* Xenochrophis.

A California kingsnake. Snakes are highly evolved animals, and the numerous types of snakes have been specialized for survival in their natural environments.

are referred to as *aglypha*, that is, their teeth do not possess grooves or hollows for the venom.

Venomous snakes are divided into three categories on the basis of their tooth structure and arrangement. First there are the *solenoglyph* snakes, which have the most highly specialized mechanism for the injection of venom. They possess in their upper jaw two greatly elongated hollow fangs which are folded into the mucous membrane of the mouth so that they lie along the upper jaw. The base of each fang is surrounded by a sheath of mucous membrane which, in turn, is connected by the venom duct to the venom gland. Snakes in this group belong to the family Viperidae (Old and New World vipers and pit vipers). When attacking, the fangs are erected, but the actual bite occasionally causes them to break off. They are then rapidly replaced by new teeth already formed in folds of the mucous membrane. In a large Gaboon viper, *Bitis gabonica*, with a length of about 15 meters, these fangs can be about four centimeters long and can inject a substantial amount of venom into prey.

The second group of venomous snakes, the *proteroglypha* (involving mostly the family Elapidae), have a pair of grooved or hollow elongated fangs attached to the front of the upper jaw. They are rigidly attached in an erect position and fit into a pocket in the outer gum of the lower jaw. These fangs are directly connected to venom glands and are particularly conspicuous in mambas and cobras. This type of fang is also replaced rapidly when lost or broken off, as indeed are all rootless teeth in reptiles.

The third type represents a very special adaptation found in the rear-fanged snakes (Boiginae) or *opisthoglypha*. This group also includes some genera of the otherwise non-venomous family of colubrid snakes (Colubridae). The fangs possess venom grooves, but only through the massaging action of chewing prey is the venom actually injected. However, since these teeth are situated far

back in the upper jaw, they are only used on fairly small prey, their natural food. Unfortunately, however, this can also involve the hobbyist's fingers. Deaths to humans through bites from these snakes have indeed been reported. A tragic example was the death of the grand old man of German herpetologists, Prof. Dr. Robert Mertens (world-renowned reptile expert and for many years director of the famous Senckenberg Museum at Frankfurt). In his old age, in 1975, he was bitten by one of the two deadly species of rear-fanged snakes, the twig snake, *Thelotornis kirtlandii*. A bite from the other equally deadly species, the boomslang, *Dispholidus typus*, proved fatal to the equally famous American herpetologist Karl P. Schmidt in 1957.

Some general remarks about venomous snakes may be relevant at this stage. Many hobbyists underestimate the danger of these animals or are under the impression that adequate antivenins are available, which then only have to be injected to render a possible bite from a venomous snake harmless. Such attitudes are totally wrong. Any bite from a venomous snake has to be viewed as a life-endangering accident and dealt with accordingly. Antivenins are not available for all species and, furthermore, the physiological responses of the bite victims may

The nominate form of the brown sand boa, Eryx johnii johnii. *Snakes of this species require a dry period of hibernation which helps stimulate breeding.*

vary from one individual to the next. Cardiac arrest (heart failure) may still set in despite an antivenin having been given. The amount of venom injected by a snake bite may exceed that required to cause death to a human by a very substantial margin. For instance, the venom of a black mamba, *Dendroaspis polylepis*, is so potent that 120mg is sufficient to kill a human, yet the snake injects about 1000mg with each bite. With some species one milligram is enough to kill, but then the amount commonly injected is correspondingly small, as in the krait, *Bungarus candidus*.

Garden tree boas grow to two meters in length. For food they may take small mammals, birds, lizards, and frogs.

Because of the elongated shape of snakes, their internal organs are adjusted accordingly in shape and position. Paired organs such as kidneys and gonads (testes and ovaries) are separated and are not at the same level. This, in fact, can lead to some asymmetry, as can be seen in the lobes of the lung. The more primitive snakes (Boidae) still have both lobes, but the left one is substantially smaller than the right one. In colubrid snakes there is essentially only the right lobe remaining or there are only very small remnants of the left lobe still visible. The extension of the lungs posteriorly varies greatly. In some species, such as the Indian rat snake,

Ptyas mucosus, or the saw-scaled viper, *Echis carinatus*, and also in truly aquatic file or wart snakes, *Acrochordus*, the lungs extend almost to the cloaca. Generally in snakes, only less than one-half of the lung participates in gas exchange. The remainder, which is in the form of membranous air sacs, functions as storage.

The shape of the snakes appears to have also caused the distant separation of the gall bladder from the liver. The esophagus leads directly into the stomach. This is followed by the small intestine, with the pancreas located in the first (duodenal) loop and the bile duct leading into it. The small intestine consists of a number of loops suspended and kept in position by mesenteries. Such an arrangement is important, since the small intestine is longer

A corn snake being probed to determine its sex. This particular snake is a male.

than the abdominal cavity. The length of the small intestine depends upon the food requirements of a snake. Differentiation into distinct sections is very difficult.

At the junction between the small intestines and the colon, there exists in the Boidae a short appendix (cecum); this is absent in all other snakes. It is difficult to determine the transition from the colon to the last portion of the digestive tract, the rectum. Since the oviduct and the sperm ducts, as well as the ureter, join this section of the digestive tract, it is generally referred to as the cloaca. The male sex organs (hemipenes) are located in pouches at the base of the tail and project from the cloaca when erected.

The circulatory system of snakes is in principle more or less identical with that of all the other reptiles. There are two aortal arches which join posteriorly to the heart to form the dorsal aorta.

Little can be said about the hearing in snakes. A tympanic membrane is absent, but all other components of the inner ear are present, as in all other reptiles. However, the distal end of that part of the inner ear bones (columella), which would ordinarily articulate with the tympanic membrane, articulates with the quadrate bone in snakes. This bone in snakes is relatively free, being only loosely attached by ligaments to the lower jaw and to the skull. Experiments have shown that, because of this arrangement, snakes can perceive extremely minute vibrations. It is, however, utter nonsense to say that a cobra moves its body in response to music from the flute of a snake charmer. In reality the snake responds to the swaying movements of the snake charmer with its own threat movements, so creating to the uninitiated the impression that these snakes can actually hear the music.

Hobbyists are no doubt familiar with the terms egg-laying (oviparous) and live-bearing (viviparous) snakes. Although these terms are commonly used to indicate two entirely different processes, in reality they are identical. In live-bearing snakes the embryonic development takes place inside eggs which remain inside the body of the female. Anybody who has ever witnessed the birth of young rainbow boas, *Epicrates cenchria*, and compared this to the hatching of egg-laying snakes will have noticed that the differences are not very significant. Even the young of live-bearing snakes have to break through their egg shell (which, however, is not calcareous and rigid) after these have emerged from the cloaca. Thus live-bearing species are more appropriately referred to as being ovoviviparous, since they reproduce by laying eggs which are ready to hatch.

An albino corn snake. As with other animals, few albino snakes are born in the wild.

This is accomplished by the internal development of the young, which receive their nourishment from the egg yolk, instead of an arrangement of placental development inside the female. It is easier for hobbyists who would like to try their hand at breeding snakes to select those which lay eggs ready to hatch, instead of the true egg-laying species.

The difficulty with oviparous eggs is to not disturb the embryonic development, which may sometimes require many weeks. If the eggs are kept too dry

MORPHOLOGY AND ECOLOGY OF SNAKES

they will shrivel up and the embryos will die; similarly, keeping eggs too cool will cause the death of the embryo. It does require a considerable amount of experience—even a good deal of luck—to provide the correct conditions for the snake eggs. Therefore, it is easier to breed live-bearing snakes, especially since a well-suited pair often reproduces repeatedly in captivity, as indeed has been reported from rainbow boas, for instance.

In order to illustrate some of the difficulties with egg-laying snakes, the following example is given. During an exhibition by a wandering reptile menagerie, a female *Python molurus bivittatus* laid eggs. As is typical for this species, the female coiled herself tightly around the eggs and maintained this position for several weeks. Through periodic contractions the female elevates the brood temperature several degrees above ambient

A female indigo snake, Drymarchon corais, with her clutch of 11 recently laid eggs. Breeding snakes requires experience in snake maintenance and a good knowledge of the species in question. Snake breeding is not recommended for the beginner.

The reticulated python has been bred in captivity, but as members of this species are egglayers, they are not as easy to breed as many ovoviviparous species. Ovoviviparity means that the eggs develop while they are within the mother's body.

temperature. In this particular instance, the snake, together with her eggs, was placed in a cage padded with straw, which then had to be left behind by the owner. This appeared to pose no problems, since the animal didn't need feeding and only drinking water had to be offered. In order to maintain the necessary humidity, an attendant frequently squirted water inside the cage. When, after about eight weeks of incubation, from 42 eggs only five eggs hatched, the owner noticed to his consternation that the female had several large, foul-smelling skin lacerations. Some ribs were exposed and bits and pieces of straw were forced between them. There was no skin left at all in these areas. What had happened? The frequent spraying of the cage with water had caused the straw to rot. This rotting eventually spread to the snake, which continued to incubate the eggs. Fortunately the snake responded well to treatment and was completely healed after a few months, so that two years later there were only scars still visible.

In any snake-breeding attempt, and this should always be the ultimate objective in animal husbandry, the hobbyist is more likely to succeed with ovoviviparous snakes.

Diseases

In this chapter some of the important snake diseases will be discussed, with emphasis upon those which the hobbyist, with the aid of proper medication, can treat himself. Therefore, by necessity this discussion has to be limited to infectious diseases involving bacteria, fungi and ectoparasites as well as mechanical injuries. Since pathological conditions involving internal organs cannot be treated by the average hobbyist, they will not be elaborated on in this text.

Any obviously diseased snake must be accommodated in a separate cage. Such a quarantine cage can be essentially bare, with the exception of a drinking container (not for bathing), a rock, possibly a climbing branch or stump and several layers of newspaper to cover the bottom. The latter has the advantage that newsprint tends to inhibit bacterial growth, and the paper absorbs moisture and can be replaced as needed. An optimal ambient temperature and humidity must also be provided. The most serious problems with snakes are gastrointestinal diseases.

MOUTH ROT

Mouth rot, a common cause of death in earlier years, has become fairly rare nowadays. It can be caused by a number of different bacteria, but most commonly members of the genus *Pseudomonas* are implicated.

Such infections occur predominantly in weakened animals, usually newly imported ones, which have not been looked after properly for quite some time. The typical symptoms are pale mouth epithelium, followed by patchy, acutely infected (pus) areas which often penetrate deep into the surrounding tissue. Treatment involves the removal—with a cotton ball or swab—of the pus and daily application or injection into the dorsal musculature of a broad-spectrum antibiotic such as terramycin, aureomycin or a suitable sulfonamide. The most effective treatment would, of course, be achieved by an exact determination of the pathogen involved through techniques unfortunately available only in a professional laboratory. This would permit the use of a specific antibiotic and eliminate all guess work.

While treating a snake for mouth rot, it is advisable to give an injectable vitamin mixture. This should include vitamin A and vitamin C. Since mucous membranes and teeth are regenerated very readily, healing takes place quite rapidly.

Opposite: A Mexican rosy boa, Lichanura trivirgata. *Good feeding practices and a clean, suitable environment will go a long way in keeping pet snakes healthy.*

DISEASES

INTERNAL PROBLEMS

Commonly observed diseases involving the gastrointestinal tract may be caused by the same pathogens affecting the oral cavity. Those usually isolated through bacteriological tests belong to the genera *Pseudomonas* and *Aeromonas*. Since only an autopsy of dead animals reveals accurately these diseases (the mucous lining of the digestive tract shows profound changes), one has to rely on symptoms (behavioral changes) of the live animal. Fishes, by the way, are subject to pathogens belonging to these same genera.

Once again, newly acquired animals are very prone to such infections. Significant symptoms are refusing food, particularly in those species which are usually very good feeders in captivity, and, more importantly, regurgitating partially digested food after a few days. The latter is indicative of the fact that the stomach can still digest food while the disease may not be too advanced. However, once a food item reaches the small intestines, reverse peristalsis sets in because of the infection of the mucous lining. This then causes the food to be thrown up. Should the sick animals still be able to pass feces from previously eaten food, this will be mushy, foul smelling and of gray coloration. Unless proper treatment is initiated immediately, the snake will die in short order.

Accurate determination of a specific antibiotic would bring the best and most immediate results; however, this could cause a serious delay. Therefore, it is best if a broad-spectrum antibiotic or a sulfonamide is given immediately. Chloromycetin (chloramphenicol) has been very effective, particularly when given directly into the stomach via a thin hose connected to a syringe. The recommended dosage is about 50mg per kilogram body weight on the first day. During the following five to seven days this can be reduced by about half of the original dose.

SALMONELLA

The feces of newly arrived snakes usually contain a high accumulation of *Salmonella*, pathogens which may include symptoms similar to food poisoning in humans. It can be shown that nearly 40% of all reptiles carry these bacteria, but most of these are part of the normal gastrointestinal microfauna and are harmless to the animals. The inherent danger of such reptilian bacteria to humans is often overestimated. This is not to disguise the fact that reptile diseases have been transmitted to humans, but such cases have been few in comparison to the number of reptiles held in captivity. Moreover, if the quarantine guidelines are being observed, there should really be no problem.

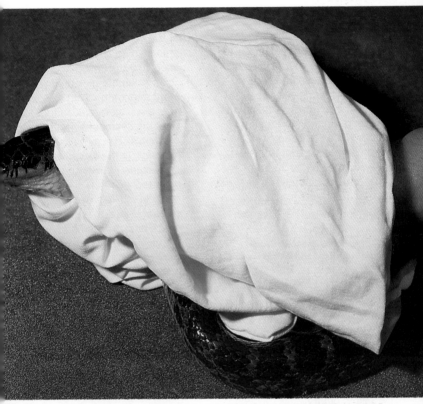

A horseshoe snake, Coluber hippocrepis, *caught for handling and inspection. Pet snakes should be observed for signs of illness, but this visual inspection need not involve overhandling the snake.*

Snakes which are known to carry *Salmonella* without any clinical disease symptoms should best be left untreated. Beyond that, it must be remembered that it is virtually impossible to remove gastrointestinal bacteria from reptiles for any length of time.

SKIN DISEASE

Skin diseases in snakes due to fungi (mycosis) have been on the increase in recent years. Rapidly enlarging brown spots, usually on the ventral scales, are symptomatic. Often such affected skin patches begin to hemorrhage and form pus. Skin diseases can spread very rapidly and can affect the entire ventral area of a snake within a few weeks. Treatment of mycosis has to be initiated early. Once again, clinically determining the correct medication would be the most effective way to treat these diseases, but this takes too much time. This then leaves only trial and error experimentation with different fungicidal agents available from most veterinarians. Only persistent and repeated application will lead to an eventually successful treatment. Fungal infections of internal organs are comparatively rare and usually do not respond satisfactorily to treatment.

PARASITES

Snakes are also prone to parasitic diseases. Parasites are those organisms which live at the expense of others. They affect a host by utilizing its food supply as well as through their excretory products, which are often poisonous to the host. The host will invariably try to develop a physiological immunity to the parasites, but it rarely succeeds. Parasitic effects to the host can range from barely noticeable to deadly. Such parasites include single-celled organisms (protozoans), worms (helminths, e.g. flatworms, trematodes, tapeworms, cestodes, roundworms, nematodes), as well as mites, ticks and tongue worms (pentastomids).

Protozoans: A serious disease is amoebiasis, which is caused by *Entamoeba invadens*. This organism exists in two different stages, one that actively feeds and reproduces, the trophozoite,

and a second form which is protected against environmental effects by becoming encysted. Snakes tend to pick up these cysts through drinking water. These will then release four to eight small amoebae in the colon of snakes. The amoebae feed on materials in the digestive tract and on bacteria. Within hours they have reached their full size and begin to multiply by simple division. Since these organisms attack mucous membrane inside the digestive tract as well as capillaries in the wall, substantial damage can be caused. They often invade adjacent tissue and spread through the blood stream to other organs. Because of the direction of blood flow, they will settle first in the liver. However, irrespective of where they settle, it always involves substantial tissue damage. Depending upon the condition and size of the snake, death may occur from 14 days to several weeks after the onset of the infection. The affected section of the digestive tract sometimes shows very characteristic layering, an indication of attempted tissue regeneration. Hobbyists once called this membranous enteritis. Snakes thus infected can be recognized by their abnormal resting posture and behavior. That is, they are stretched out, drink a lot and refuse to feed.

Occasionally, bloody feces are excreted. On the ventral side of the snake's body, in the anterior

Liasis mackloti, *Macklot's python. This species is a forest dweller in its natural habitat. It is not recommended for beginners.*

area of the cloaca, one can feel a hard lump several centimeters long. Without proper treatment such an animal will invariably die. In the early stages of the disease, treatment with some of the newer types of medication is rather effective. At the same time, tablets introduced directly into the cloaca have further improved the effectiveness of the treatment.

Only strict compliance with quarantine measures will prevent this disease from spreading to other animals.

Helminths: Parasitic worms in snakes are fairly common. However, if treatment is to be effective, the type of worm involved has to be determined. This can easily be done by examining the feces. If cestodes (tapeworms) seem to be implicated, the feces when dissolved in water will release some of the segments. Trematodes, which can be found in many snakes, occur in the large intestine, the gall bladder or the gall bladder ducts, as well as in the kidney and its ducts. Trematode infestations are not particularly rare, but since their treatment is fairly difficult, it need not be given further consideration here.

The life cycle of these worms invariably involves an intermediate host other than a snake. Therefore, it is impossible for these worms to spread within a terrarium situation. More important are tapeworms, which, as sexually reproducing stages, may occur in large numbers in the digestive tract and have a detrimental effect upon the snake. In any event, one should attempt to get rid of these worms, something which is dependent upon an exact determination of the worm species involved.

Two types of medication can be selected for treatment of cestode infestations. The older one, derived from human medicine, which unfortunately may have some adverse effects on some snakes (e.g. *Natrix natrix*), must be given orally (for *Bothridium* at least twice) in a dosage of from 150-200mg per kilogram body weight. A somewhat newer medication, requiring only a single oral dose of 2-5mg per kilogram body weight, is sufficient for all tapeworms except *Bothridium* and related forms. For these, a dosage of 25-30mg per kilogram body weight is required.

Like trematodes, cestodes also present no danger of transmission

A viperine water snake, Natrix maura. *Captive snakes are prone to skin diseases; therefore, the proper cage conditions with regard to humidity and cage bottom material are important.*

It is a good idea to clean cage furnishings periodically and to keep an eye out for any signs of snake parasites.

to other snakes in the same cage since they also require several intermediate hosts to successfully complete their life cycle. However, since some snakes themselves are intermediate hosts for these worms, reaching their final stage in birds of prey or carnivorous mammals, certain worm stages may occur occasionally in some snakes. For instance, the second larval stage (pleroceroid) of pseudophyllid tapeworms often occurs on long (several centimeters), thread-like, intertwined aggregations in the musculature between the ribs of a snake. They can be detected from the outside as soft lumps and

should be removed via a small incision into the skin of the animal. An antibiotic powder applied to the wound will invariably speed up healing.

Snakes can also be intermediate hosts for the larvae known as *tetrathyridia*, which occur in the abdominal or gastrointestinal walls. Just like the similar spiny-headed worms (acanthocephalids), these tapeworm larvae cannot be effectively removed.

Far more significant are the roundworms (nematodes) which occur in a large number of snakes. For the hobbyist the worms which inhabit the gastrointestinal tract are the more important ones, since they can be treated very effectively. More difficult to get rid of are the nematodes which attack the lungs and other tissue areas, such as the medina worms (dracunculids), or those invading tissue and blood vessels, the filariids. These nematodes are not only difficult to detect but virtually impossible to get rid of without adversely affecting the snake, too.

Particularly important are the large threadworm species which can cause inflammation in the stomach walls and lead to the death of the host. The eggs of these worms are very characteristic and easily recognizable. Other species, which belong in the order Strongylida (bursa nematodes), sometimes occur in large numbers in the esophagus or the large intestine. These are usually small to medium-size worms. The presence of lung nematodes can be detected by motile first stage larvae in freshly excreted feces or in oral mucus.

Treatment of nematodes in the digestive tract is fairly easy with some of the widely available broad-spectrum antihelminthic agents. Several are commonly available in pet shops. Particularly effective—in small dosages— against most nematodes, yet completely harmless to the host, are those administered orally; a single dose of 30 to 50mg per kilogram is usually successful. In more persistent cases, as, for instance, with hairworms, Capillaria, a daily dose of 20 to 30mg per kilogram of body weight, given over an eight to ten day period, will lead to an elimination of the worms. Similarly effective, but in larger dosages only, are those agents containing mebendazole. These are usually given in dosages of 100mg per kilogram of body weight for one to three days.

Vermicides, which have to be applied only once, are easily administered to feeding snakes via their food. In other cases, the drug has to be dissolved or diluted in water and then given via a thin tube directly into the stomach. Such a tube should be lubricated with egg white and then, with twisting and massaging motions, gently slid down into the stomach.

Microscopic examinations of the feces sometimes reveal some strange eggs which contain fully developed larvae with vestigial appendages and two hooks each. These are the so-called tongue worms (pentastomids) which, during their reproductive stage, inhabit the respiratory tract of snakes. Taxonomically these parasitic worms are related to the centipedes and millipedes, and sometimes they reach rather substantial sizes. They can cause an infectious pneumonia which may lead to the death of the host. There is, unfortunately, no known treatment available.

...ather dark reticulated python. All newly imported snakes should be checked for ...s and mites, which should be promptly removed and their bites treated with the ...per medication.

Arthropods: In this phylum ...ly native mites and ticks *...carii)*—apart from the previously ...scussed pentastomids—are ...gnificant snake parasites. Nearly ... newly imported snakes carry ...ks. These have to be removed, ...nce they can develop into plague ...oportions under the favorable ...nditions of a terrarium. Usually ...ks can be removed manually. ...ey are grasped with forceps ...d through repeated semi-...rcular motions, which will cause ...e embedded mouth parts to be ...leased, can be gently pulled off. ...ost ticks parasitizing snakes ...long to the family Ixodidae. ...ach tick bite should be treated ...th an antibiotic ointment in order

to prevent bacterial infection. This commonly occurs if the tick's mouth parts remain in the snake and inflammatory tissue response ejects these particles.

Even more dangerous than ixodid ticks are those belonging to the family Argasidae. Of these, only the tiny, earliest larval stages (six-legged larvae) live for a few days under the snake's scales and suck blood. The more advanced larval form and the sexually reproducing adults (eight legs) remain hidden under stones, rocks, tree bark, etc. and thus go unnoticed. Blood is sucked for about 20-30 minutes at night. These ticks are particularly dangerous since they suck

63

DISEASES

sufficient blood from young snakes to kill them. In addition, they are known to be carriers of filariid roundworms. The elimination of these ticks is rather difficult, and only regular inspections and manual removal, as well as repeated sterilization of the cage, can eventually eliminate the problem.

Special agents to remove mites and ticks (acaricides) are commercially available, but they are not 100% effective, particularly against argasids. In addition, they are rather poisonous to many snakes.

Far more common than ticks are blood mites of the genera *Ophionyssus* and *Liponyssus*. They are blood-sucking, only about 1mm in length, and under favorable conditions can reproduce themselves to enormous numbers within a few weeks. Attacked snakes look like they are covered with thousands of little black dots, interspersed with tiny white ones, the excretory products of the mites. The constant loss of blood in young snakes can lead to rapid death. Unlike lizards, which can remove such parasites with their mouths, affected snakes prefer to spend long periods of time in a water bath, which afterward is covered by thousands of dead mites. Unfortunately, not all mites are killed this way. Those attached around the eyes and in the nasal passages, as well as the eggs located under the scales and throughout the cage, survive and form the basis for another rapidly increasing population explosion of mites.

There is no general, all-around effective treatment method against mites since species react rather differently. A method we found rather effective involved spraying white cotton bags with a 0.2% solution of neguvon. These bags were subsequently permitted to dry again. The mite-infested snakes were placed inside these bags for several hours, perhaps even overnight. The even distribution of the substance over the entire bag, together with the movement of the snakes, gave maximum exposure to the mites, of which there were thousands found dead in the bag after the treatment. We consider this method to be more effective than direct spraying of the animals, since this has been observed to lead to poisoning symptoms among the treated snakes. Even more dangerous is bathing the snakes in this solution.

Any treatment must, of course, be accompanied by a thorough cleaning (washing out with some acaricide agent) of the cage and an equally thorough rinsing out afterward. All previous cage decorations should be destroyed by burning.

Another possibility in dealing with mites has come about more recently through the use of

64

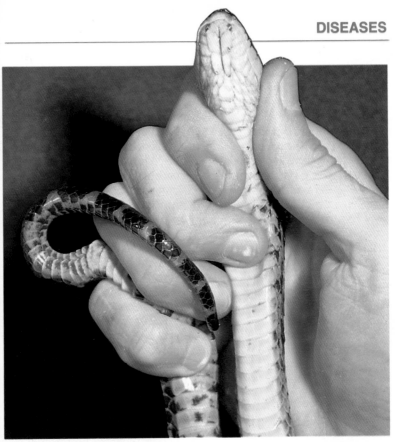

Whenever it is necessary to handle a snake, take advantage of the opportunity to check its underside for parasites.

commercially available insecticide strips. These can be placed directly into large cages or, in the case of several smaller cages, in the same room. Trial and error methods will determine the correct and most effective exposure length. It is important, however, to start out with short periods, which can be extended if, after the previous exposures, mites are still around 24 hours after the strip has been removed. Caution is far better than to encounter losses among the snakes. This method works only in dry cages which have a relatively low humidity.

Incomplete removal of ticks, as well as bites from food animals, can lead to infections in snakes and should be treated with antibiotic ointment or powder. Scars from earlier wounds and injuries will disappear after several months.

Easy-to-Keep Snake Species

This chapter is somewhat difficult for me to formulate, since the term easy-to-keep has only relative meaning in relationship to the experience of the individual hobbyist. For instance, one hobbyist may have kept a certain snake species quite satisfactorily for many years, while another one may have had consistently bad luck with the same species. A good example is the emerald tree boa, *Corallus caninus*, which is considered by most hobbyists to be difficult at best and with a longevity of one year considered to be a success. Yet Henri Watzer, an experienced Swiss hobbyist, has kept a specimen for more than 13 years. There are many such examples, so the content of this chapter will most likely not be mutually agreed upon by all.

However, in assessing different successes (and failures), a number of different factors have to be taken into consideration. The most important prerequisite for successful acclimation is that a newly imported snake arrives in optimum condition. Beyond that, those species which have rather specific requirements, as for instance the emerald tree boa, which in the wild rests hanging from a branch, has to be packed singly for shipment and not stuffed into a sack with several other snakes. Another important point is that the snake be offered cage conditions compatible with its ecological requirements. Furthermore, all measures described in the chapters on quarantine and diseases have to be carefully complied with.

I consider the species listed below as being easy to keep, a general judgment based upon my own years of experience as well as those of hobbyists who have passed them on to me for this purpose. Nevertheless, the selection of snakes listed below must remain subjective, and some experienced hobbyist may find his particular choice as an easily kept snake missing from this tabulation.

For easy reference, the various ecological requirements which have to be considered in setting up a cage for a specific snake species are set out below. It must be kept in mind that these are merely basic types of cage or terrarium set-ups which may have to receive further modification to meet specific requirements for certain species.

ECOLOGICAL CHARACTERISTICS OF A SNAKE CAGE (TERRARIUM)

Dry terrarium: Only drinking

Opposite: A young reticulated python. The proper cage ecology is most important for successful snake keeping. Different species have different needs with regard to temperature, humidity, and furnishings.

water container required. Sand as substrate, as well as some large rough and smooth rocks. Climbing facilities not needed (e.g. sand boa, *Eryx*).

Moist terrarium: Requires large water container, ample plant growth and climbing facilities. Moss as substrate on top of humus soil or peat moss. Humidity 50-80% (e.g. garter snakes, *Thamnophis*; European grass or water snake, *Natrix natrix*; emerald tree boa, *Corallus caninus*; and others).

Semi-moist terrarium: Large water container required, loose top soil or peat moss, slightly wetted down. Climbing facilities not absolutely necessary (e.g. pipe snakes, *Cylindrophis*).

Basic terrarium: Water container sufficiently large for bathing; large, rough rocks or stones needed, substrate to consist of pea-size gravel or pebbles; climbing branches. For esthetics, plants can be added (various boas, pythons and slender boas, *Epicrates*).

Temperature ranges: Snakes which come from tropical latitudes should have a daytime temperature of about 28°C (82°F), which can drop down to 22–25°C (72–77°F) at night. Snakes from temperate latitudes should be given temperatures which do not exceed 22–24°C (72–75°F) during the day; at night the temperature may drop down to 16-18°C (60–65°F).

PIPE SNAKES
FAMILY ANILIIDAE
Cylindrophus rufus, **Red Pipe Snake**

TERRARIUM: Semi-moist, 28°C day, 22-25°C night

SIZE: to about 70cm

DISTRIBUTION: Southeast Asia, commonly in rice paddies, burrowing down to 50cm in mud.

HUSBANDRY: Loose top soil containing decaying leaves (humus), at least 10cm deep; water container sufficiently large for bathing. Since feces are deposited in soil, substrate has to be replaced often. This snake is recommended for experienced hobbyists only, who wish to make specific observations, since it stays underground except when feeding.

FOOD: Small live fish which are caught by the snake; lizards, geckos, small snakes.

OTHER SPECIES: *Cylindrophis maculatus* (care and maintenance as above).

Beautifully iridescent skin, dorsally uniformly dark gray to black, irregular white cross bands ventrally. The short tip of the tail is orange-red underneath, and when frightened the tail is whipped up. This reaction causes the snake's body to become substantially flattened.

GIANT SNAKES
FAMILY BOIDAE

When discussing these snakes, reference must be made to the

The boa constrictor should have water available for both drinking and bathing, and it should have a cage that provides suitable places to hide.

strict import regulations under the *Washington Agreement for the Protection of Endangered Species*. Although these snakes are referred to as the giant snakes, only a few species actually deserve this title. However, since their morphological characteristics and feeding behavior are identical, such a grouping seems justified.

Boid snakes kill their prey by means of a lightning fast strike, grabbing the prey with their teeth and simultaneously wrapping themselves around and strangling the prey (another name for them is the constrictors). As soon as cardiac arrest has set in, the snake loosens its stranglehold and its bite, and then, gliding its tongue over the prey, distinguishes head from tail. The rapid tongue movements fan the odor molecules to the roof of the oral cavity. Each time the forked tongue is retracted the tips are inserted into a paired vomeronasal organ, Jacobson's organ, which opens into the mouth. Jacobson's organ is an accessory olfactory organ which can detect chemical substances in the air. Therefore, the tongue flicking indicates that the snake is tasting the air.

When the snake has found the head of its prey, the mouth is opened and the prey is grasped with the teeth. This is followed by swallowing the prey through alternate projections and retractions of the upper and lower jaw bones. It is important that the snake finds the head, because only in the direction of hairs or feathers can prey be swallowed without difficulties. Young snakes are sometimes so eager to feed that they get head and tail mixed up, and it requires enormous efforts then to bring the food back up and start over again, this time head first.

The most difficult part of the task is done once the head of the prey has reached the upper part of the esophagus. From there on, muscle action, noticeable by the wavelike motions of the neck, transports the food to the stomach.

Colubrid snakes (family Colubridae) rarely constrict their prey; instead it is swallowed alive. In those snakes belonging to the opisthoglypha (rear-fanged snakes), there is the added reaction to the venom once the prey has reached the upper rear fangs. The venomous Elapidae,

as well as the vipers, pit vipers and adders (Viperidae), kill their prey by a rapid strike. The specialized venom fangs in the upper jaw inject the venom, which kills the prey. Only after it is dead will it be swallowed.

SUBFAMILY BOIDAE
NEW WORLD BOAS

(All are ovoviviparous)
***Boa constrictor*, Boa constrictor**

TERRARIUM: Basic, 28°C day 22-25°C night

SIZE: to three meters, juveniles 50-60cm

DISTRIBUTION: Mexico to northern Argentina.

FOOD: Young snakes will take small mice, but will soon accept medium size food; after six to eight months fully grown mice and young rats can be taken. Larger boas (1-1.2m length) will also eagerly take newly hatched chicks, young pigeons, etc. Frequent feedings will result in fairly rapid growth.

Due to unsuitable transport conditions, these snakes often suffer considerable losses. Unfortunately, mortalities usually do not set in until the snakes are already with the hobbyist. Newly imported juveniles are particularly prone to bacterial gastrointestinal diseases. Healthy specimens usually feed well in captivity and under suitable conditions will reproduce. Because of increasingly severe import

Although it is basically a ground-dwelling snake, the cage of the rainbow boa should contain rocks or branches for climbing.

restrictions, hobbyists should be advised to acquire this snake in pairs. Males are more slender and have longer rear "claws" than females. According to many hobbyists, boas belong to those snakes which become relatively tame. While young specimens are fairly aggressive, they will adjust rapidly to handling by hobbyists—but these snakes are never children's toys!!

Epicrates cenchria, **Rainbow Boa**

TERRARIUM: Basic, 28°C day 22-25°C night

SIZE: to about 1-5m

DISTRIBUTION: Widely distributed throughout South and Central America; the only species of this genus which inhabits the mainland.

FOOD: Mice, rats, possibly chicks.

OTHER SPECIES: *Epicrates angulifer*, Cuban boa, island species which grows up to 4.5m; not easily kept in captivity. Several other Caribbean species.

Conspicuously iridescent skin (particularly after a recent molt). The cage must contain ample climbing opportunities. Hobbyists lucky enough to be able to breed this snake will be fascinated by the breaking through of young from their fetal membrane immediately after these have been deposited by the mother. A remnant umbilical connection to the (former) egg yolk will remain visible on the ventral side of the snakes. Usually not all newly hatched boas will take food on their own within ten to 14 days; sometimes force-feeding once or twice with newly born (pink) mice is necessary.

Corallus enydris, Garden Tree Boa

TERRARIUM: Basic, 28°C day 22-25°C night

SIZE: in excess of 2m

DISTRIBUTION: Northern South America, including large areas of Brazil.

Requires ample climbing facilities. A subspecies, *C. enydris cookii*, Cook's tree boa, grows to only about 1.5m. This snake can be kept rather well in a combination of terrarium types (moist and basic), and it has a unique climbing technique whereby it can move about on thin vertical branches without any problems. The resting place is usually on horizontal branches in a very characteristic coiled position with the head on top. Care of this snake requires some experience, yet it is possible to breed garden tree boas in captivity for several generations.

Eunectes murinus, Anaconda

TERRARIUM: Basic, 28°C day 22-25°C night

SIZE: 6m, maximum 8m

DISTRIBUTION: In water (rivers, lakes, swamps, etc.) over wide areas of South America.

FOOD: All kinds of small mammals and birds, sometimes takes fish; large specimens should be fed fully grown chickens, ducks and rabbits.

OTHER SPECIES: *Eunectes notaeus*, the yellow or Paraguay anaconda, lives in southern South American rivers and grows to 2m; lighter coloration than *E. murinus*, easy to keep. Very rare, endangered species; importation prohibited.

Requires large water basin for bathing. Juveniles are particularly suitable for hobbyists. If not fed excessively, this snake can be kept for many years in a medium-sized cage. Only rarely will an anaconda lose its aggressiveness. Characterized by a gray-green coloration with dark gray to black patches.

Sanzinia madagascariensis, Madagascar Tree Boa

TERRARIUM: Basic, 28°C day 22-25°C night

SIZE: rarely larger than 2m

DISTRIBUTION: Madagascar.

Intensive gray-green coloration with many dark spots; difficult for beginners to keep, but experienced hobbyists may be able to keep it for many years. Exportation prohibited.

Headstudy of a yellow anaconda, Eunectes notaeus. *Anacondas require substantial water areas and warm, dry spots on which to dry themselves.*

Eryx johnii, Brown Sand Boa

TERRARIUM: Dry, 28°C day 22-25°C night

DISTRIBUTION: Middle East to India.

FOOD: Small rodents, lizards.

OTHER SPECIES: *Eryx jaculus,* javelin sand boa. Occurs throughout southeastern Europe, Middle East, North Africa. Small species; grows to 60cm; nicely colored with attractive spots. Rarely available commercially.

Other genera in this subfamily, such as *Lichanura* (North America) or *Candoia* (East Asia, Pacific islands), are equally rarely available. Authenticated reports indicate that these snakes are considerably more difficult to keep than *Eryx.*

The brown sand boa is an Old World burrowing boa, very agile, with a short stout head barely distinguishable from rest of body. This snake appears plump, but can move about quite rapidly. It sometimes attempts to bite when being handled. Can be kept easily, but only of interest to specialist hobbyists, since it rarely stays above ground. The skin is uniformly sand-colored. Needs very little water. When kept in a cage with dry coarse sand, molting is rarely a problem.

SUBFAMILY PYTHONINAE OLD WORLD PYTHONS

Some of the most popular snakes for hobbyists belong to this group. Although most of them grow to very substantial sizes, they are common in the cages of hobbyists because they are easily kept. However, not all species have a placid temperament. They are found in the Old World (Africa, southeast Asia and Australia). All pythons lay eggs which are, with few exceptions, incubated.

Python reticulatus, Reticulated Python

TERRARIUM: Basic, 28°C day 22-25°C night

SIZE: 5-6m

DISTRIBUTION: Southeast Asia, Indo-Australian archipelago.

A Madagascar tree boa. This species does well in a tall terrarium that is provided with adequate ventilation.

A javelin sand boa, Eryx jaculus. *As* Eryx *species are burrowing ground-dwellers, their cages should contain sufficient amounts of bottom material into which they can dig.*

FOOD: Juveniles will take all small rodents as well as birds; large specimens feed on rabbits, ducks, etc.

Attractively marked, but excessive hunting for leather has severely depleted this species, and large specimens are rarely encountered in the wild any more. The eggs are about 6cm long, from which juveniles with a length of about 60cm hatch. At hatching the snakes are very slender and weigh nearly 100g. Their food drive is enormous, so it is not uncommon to see them grow at a rate of about 50cm per year, with a corresponding weight gain. Therefore, cages to accommodate young pythons have to be sufficiently large since a length of 3m is easily reached within five years. They are robust and interesting snakes, but most specimens remain rather aggressive. Any hobbyist who keeps this species for any length of time will sooner or later encounter its teeth, sunk into a hand or an arm. Therefore, it is strongly recommended that this snake, and, for that matter, all other giant snakes, not be handled by a single person. The danger of being strangled is simply too great, and the teeth can be 1cm in length!

Python molurus, Asiatic Rock Python

TERRARIUM: Basic, 28°C day 22-25°C night

SIZE: 3-5m

DISTRIBUTION: Large areas of southeast Asia.

FOOD: Not particular; mammals and birds. Juvenile specimens take small rodents and newly hatched chicks; adult snakes feed on guinea pigs, rabbits, fully grown chickens, ducks, sometimes even on piglets.

Occurs as two subspecies: *P. molurus molurus*, the light rock python (totally protected), and *P. molurus bivittatus*, the dark rock python (rarely available commercially). Not very demanding when kept in captivity.

Python sebae, African Rock Python

TERRARIUM: Basic, 28°C day 22-25°C night

SIZE: rarely more than 4m, occasionally up to 6.5m

DISTRIBUTION: Africa south of the Sahara Desert.

FOOD: Larger mammals and birds.

Not only confined to rocky areas, but also occurs in bushland, sometimes even in forests. This snake is intensively hunted by natives for food and leather, which has reduced its numbers significantly. It is rarely available commercially. *Python*

sebae adjusts well to captivity; some specimens become relatively tame while others remain aggressive.

Liasis amethistinus, Amethyst Python

TERRARIUM: Basic, 28°C day 22-25°C night

SIZE: to about 6.5m

DISTRIBUTION: Australian region in areas overgrown with mangroves.

FOOD: Pigeons, chickens, subadult ducks, mammals.

OTHER SPECIES: In the same distribution area occurs the brown water python, *Liasis fuscus*. Its dorsal side is dark olive-green to brown, and the ventral side is bright yellow-green. The spotted or Children's python, *L. childreni*, has, in contrast to the other species, a distinct patchy pattern. Both species do well in captivity, where they prefer moist surroundings. These species eat rodents, according to the size of the snake to be fed.

The amethyst python requires a large bathing container and high relative humidity. Its coloration is uniformly grayish brown.

COLUBRID SNAKES
FAMILY COLUBRIDAE

This is the largest family of snakes. All members in this group are characterized by their slender body and more or less agile movements. Among these snakes

An amethyst python, Liasis amethistinus. *This species requires moist surroundings, as its natural habitat is mangrove forests.*

are species of aglypha as well as opisthoglypha (rear-fanged snakes). Some of the latter can be dangerous to humans. Rear-fanged snakes are particularly treacherous, since they hang on to prey—and possibly even the hobbyist's finger—once it has been grasped. They then immediately begin to chew, which massages the venom, injected by grooved fangs in the rear of the mouth, into the tissue.

TRUE COLUBRID SNAKES
SUBFAMILY COLUBRINAE

Boaedon lineatus, African House Snake

TERRARIUM: Basic, 28°C day 22-25°C night

SIZE: to about 1m

DISTRIBUTION: Africa; close to human habitation.

FOOD: Rodents, such as rats and mice.

Uniform brown-black coloration. Very successfully kept in captivity,

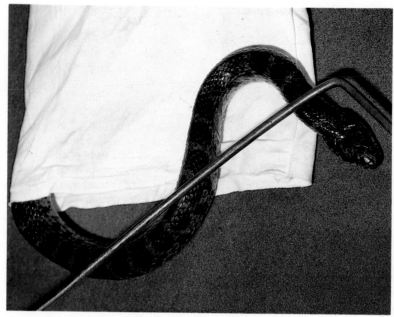

A horseshoe snake pictured with a typical sack used for transporting captured snakes and a rod used to remove the snakes from the bag.

but rarely available.

Coluber gemonensis, Arrow Racer.

TERRARIUM: Basic, 22-24°C day 16-18°C night

SIZE: to little more than 1m

DISTRIBUTION: Over wide areas of southern Europe.

FOOD: Mice, young birds, also grasshoppers.

Not well suited for captivity, since it is rather nervous and easily provoked into thrashing into the sides of the cage, inflicting injuries upon itself. Can only be kept in a large cage with many hiding places.

Coluber hippocrepis, Horseshoe Snake

TERRARIUM: Basic, 28°C day 22-25°C night

SIZE: 1.7m

DISTRIBUTION: Mediterranean region, particularly North Africa.

FOOD: Rodents.

Aggressive and always ready to bite, yet can be kept well in captivity. Strong food drive. With sufficient food this snake will reach maturity in about three years. It is popular because of its attractive markings. It requires a large cage and, when being fed, a hobbyist with a steady hand!!

Drymarchon corais, Indigo Snake

TERRARIUM: Basic, 28°C day 22-25°C night

SIZE: More than 2m

DISTRIBUTION: Southern United States and Central America southward into Brazil.

FOOD: Mammals and birds, occasionally fish. Will also feed on smaller reptiles, including snakes, if these are kept in the same cage. Captured prey is pressed against the substrate and swallowed while being entwined by the snake. If necessary, well-acclimated indigo snakes will sometimes take dead food animals.

Shiny blue-black coloration. Easily kept, but requires a suitably large cage with bathing container.

ELAPHE SPECIES
RAT SNAKES

Most of these keep well in captivity but like to climb. They are distributed over wide regions of the Old and New World. Some are colored with bright spots or patches, while others have only a dark longitudinal stripe. The cage should rather be higher than wide and provide ample climbing opportunities, such as robust plants, branches, etc. A sufficiently large water basin for complete immersion, since these snakes like to drink, should be provided and the water replaced daily. All *Elaphe* kill their prey (birds and rodents) by constriction in a manner somewhat different

from that described for the giant snakes.

Elaphe longissima, Aesculapian Snake

TERRARIUM: Basic, 22-28°C day 16-25°C night

SIZE: barely 1.8m

DISTRIBUTION: Southern Europe to the Middle East.

FOOD: Birds, also mammals according to size of snake.

This snake adapts well to captivity; cage must be equipped with plenty of climbing opportunities and a bathing container. Has been bred in captivity. Clutches consist of 6-18 eggs which hatch in about two months. Newly hatched snakes are about 20cm long.

Elaphe quatuorlineata, Four-lined Snake

TERRARIUM: Basic, 22-24°C day 16-18°C night

SIZE: more than 2m

DISTRIBUTION: Southern Europe, east of Italy.

FOOD: Rodents, newly hatched chickens.

Easily kept (the author has kept a specimen for more than eight years).

Elaphe obsoleta, Rat Snake

TERRARIUM: Basic, 28°C day 22-25°C night

SIZE: More than 2m

DISTRIBUTION: Eastern United States.

FOOD: Rodents and birds.

Elaphe guttata, Corn Snake

TERRARIUM: Basic, 28°C day 22-25°C night

SIZE: About 1.2m

DISTRIBUTION: Large areas of the United States, commonly in grain fields.

FOOD: Mice and young rats.

Attractively marked snake; has repeatedly been bred in captivity.

Elaphe situla, Leopard Snake

TERRARIUM: Basic, 22-24°C day 16-18°C night

SIZE: to about 1m

DISTRIBUTION: Southern Europe (Italy, Yugoslavia, Bulgaria to the Crimean Peninsula).

FOOD: Mice.

Beautiful spotted pattern. Only experienced herpetologists have successfully kept this snake, so it is for advanced hobbyists only.

KINGSNAKES

Lampropeltis triangulum, Milk Snake

TERRARIUM: Basic, 22-28°C day 16-25°C night

SIZE: 1-1.2m

DISTRIBUTION: North America.

FOOD: Rodents, birds, small snakes (venomous and non-venomous).

Mature adults with red and black saddles against a gray to yellow body color; juvenile colors sometimes different.

Lampropeltis getulus, Common King Snake

TERRARIUM: Basic, 28°C day 22-25°C night

SIZE: to 1.4m

DISTRIBUTION: North America.

FOOD: Rodents, reptiles (therefore, other reptiles do not belong in the same cage); is

reported to have occasionally accepted dead food animals.

Newly captured specimens are rather aggressive, but they adapt well to captivity.

NATRIX SPECIES
WATER SNAKES

A large genus containing many species which live in proximity to water but are not necessarily aquatic. They require a moist terrarium, but the cage should contain a separate dry area. Area of cage should be greater than its height.

Water snakes primarily eat fish and amphibians, but will also take lizards and skinks; young specimens feed on tadpoles, insects, even snails. Because of this type of food the feces of *Natrix* species are soft, with a penetrating smell. This requires frequent cleaning of the cage. When handled, many species will excrete a special substance from their cloacal glands, which even thorough washing does not remove.

Natrix natrix, European Grass Snake

TERRARIUM: Semi-moist, 22-24°C day 16-18°C night

DISTRIBUTION: Europe, becoming rare in heavily populated areas of central Europe.

SIZE: Females sometimes considerably longer than 1m.

FOOD: Frogs, toads, occasionally small freshwater fish; avoid perch (*Perca*) because of

A fish snake. As its common name suggests, this species primarily eats fish.

their dorsal spines; mice.

Beginning hobbyists should be discouraged from starting with this species, which is becoming increasingly rare. The nominate form of this species, *Natrix natrix natrix*, nearly always has two characteristic crescent-shaped pale yellow spots behind the head. The subspecies *Natrix natrix* *helvetica*, which grows to about 2m, has a series of small black spots on the sides of the head and body.

Natrix maura, Viperine Water Snake

TERRARIUM: Semi-moist, 22-24°C day 16-18°C night

SIZE: Less than 1m, males only to 80cm

Above: *The amethyst python is from the Australia-New Guinea area, and it may grow as large as 17 feet in length.* **Below:** *Children's python, Liasis childreni, is restricted to Australia. This species has a pattern which is more conspicuously spotted than those of its relatives.*

Above: *The arrow snake,* Coluber gemonensis, *is found in southern Europe.* **Below:** *The horseshoe snake, like other members of the genus* Coluber, *is often quite aggressive.*

DISTRIBUTION: Southwestern region of Switzerland, Italy, southern France, North Africa.

FOOD: Fish, rarely frogs, earthworms; will also take dead fish.

Zig-zag band on back, dorsal side gray-brown to olive-green.

Natrix tesselata, Dice Snake or Tessellated Snake

TERRARIUM: Semi-moist 22-24°C day 16-18°C night

SIZE: In Europe barely 1m, up to 1-5m in the Orient

DISTRIBUTION: Central and southern Europe to western China and northwest India; found only occasionally in Germany.

FOOD: Fish, amphibians.

Natrix piscator, Fish Snake

TERRARIUM: Semi-moist, 28°C day 22-24°C night

SIZE: to about 1.2m

DISTRIBUTION: Southern and southeast Asia, including East Indies.

FOOD: Fish, amphibians.

Hobbyist must be cautious when acquiring this species. Hard to acclimate since many specimens become parasitized and weakened during transport and often do not survive for very long. Healthy specimens are quite robust.

Natrix sipedon, Common Water Snake

TERRARIUM: Semi-moist, 22-24°C day 16-18°C

SIZE: to 1.3m

DISTRIBUTION: Southern Canada, southward into large areas of the United States.

FOOD: Fish.

When handled, this snake will excrete a liquid with a penetrating garlic-like odor from its cloaca.

Pseudapsis cana, Mole Snake

TERRARIUM: Basic, 28°C day 22-25°C night

SIZE: to about 1.5m

DISTRIBUTION: Southern Africa.

FOOD: Rodents.

Grayish to black snake which adapts well to captivity and may even breed. Each birth produces a large number of juveniles. Only rarely available commercially. The substrate must consist of loose sand, since this snake likes to burrow.

Ptyas mucosus, Indian Rat Snake

TERRARIUM: Basic, 28°C day 22-25°C night

SIZE: 2.5m

DISTRIBUTION: Southeast Asia.

FOOD: Practically all rodents, birds, amphibians.

Inconspicuously colored; anterior part of body brownish, posterior part appears striped or banded because of rows of blackish scales. Breeding in captivity of this egg-laying snake is not known, but should be possible. Cage should be roomy, contain a water bath and provide climbing opportunities.

Spilotes pullatus, Tropical Rat Snake

TERRARIUM: Basic, 28°C day 22-25°C night

The tropical rat snake is an excellent swimmer; therefore, an adequate bathing area is recommended.

SIZE: to about 3m

DISTRIBUTION: Brazil, humid bush environment.

FOOD: Birds, also rodents.

Jet-black with bright yellow spots and patches, predominantly ventrally. Can be kept for many years, but remains aggressive.

THAMNOPHIS SPECIES GARTER SNAKES

TERRARIUM: Moist, 28°C day 22-25°C night

SIZE: Usually between 50-70cm, rarely above 1m, with very few exceptions to 1.5m

DISTRIBUTION: North America.

FOOD: Small fish, amphibians, large earthworms.

Very nicely colored snakes which are characterized by yellow dorsal and lateral bands, which may have red or reddish-brown margins. Easily kept in captivity. Raising newly hatched juveniles presents no problems. It is important that the cage be set up in such a manner that the animals have a moist, humid environment, but a separate dry area for resting and sleeping must be provided. If these requirements are ignored, the animals become prone to skin diseases.

Above: Milk snakes are small burrowing kingsnakes. They were formerly known as Lampropeltis doliata, but their species name is now Lampropeltis triangulum. **Below:** Rat snakes are quite popular in captivity and may often be found in pet shops.

Above: The attractive coloration and easy adjustment to captivity make the corn snake a popular species with hobbyists. *Below:* The mangrove snake, Boiga dendrophila, is a highly venomous rear-fanged snake that should not be kept in captivity.

Hard-to-Keep Snakes

The accompanying list of snake species indicates which cannot be kept very well (or only with great difficulties) in captivity. Consequently they should most certainly be avoided by the beginning hobbyist. Furthermore, this list should lessen the demand (and cut the importation) of such species, with an aim toward conservation of snakes. At the same time, it protects the beginning hobbyist from acquiring snakes with which he can only have bad luck and which might well discourage him from his hobby.

Within the limited space available, it is impossible to state all reasons why a particular species is difficult to keep. Mildly venomous snakes, which are also listed here, are indicated with an * (rear-fanged snakes). Those venomous snakes (species or entire families) which can cause death among humans are marked **, despite the fact that some of them do not present any problems in their care and maintenance. Some species of venomous snakes can be kept in a terrarium, but for most hobbyists they are far too dangerous. Therefore, only those commonly available are listed. Coral and Cobra Snakes (Family Elapidae) are dangerous to extremely dangerous. Sea snakes (Family Hydrophiidae) are venomous, highly dangerous snakes which cannot be kept satisfactorily in captivity.

FAMILY TYPHLOPIDAE, Blind or Worm Snakes
FAMILY LEPTOTYPHLOPIDAE, Worm Snakes
FAMILY BOIDAE, Giant Snakes
Subfamily Boinae, New World and Madagascar Boas
Corallus caninus, Emerald Tree Boa
Lichanura roseofusca, Rosy Boa or California Boa
Subfamily Pythoninae, Old World and Australian Pythons
Aspidites species, Black-headed Python
Chondropython viridis, Green Python
Liasis albertisii, De'Albert's Python
Liasis mackloti
Morelia species, Carpet and Diamond Pythons
Python curtus, Blood Python
Python regius, Ball or King Python
FAMILY ACROCHORDIDAE
Acrocordus species, Wart or File Snakes
FAMILY COLUBRIDAE, Colubrid Snakes
Subfamily Colubrinae, True Colubrid Snakes
Coronella austriaca, Smooth Snake

Opposite: *The blood python,* Python curtus, *is the most difficult to keep of the* Python *species.*

Above: A subspecies of the European grass snake, Natrix natrix helvetica. *This snake is also known as the ringelnatter.* **Below:** An unusually yellow tropical rat snake. Most Spilotes pullatus *snakes have much smaller yellow spots.*

Above: *A pair of boomslangs,* Dispholidus typus. *Boomslangs are venomous snakes, and, therefore, they are not recommended for keeping in captivity.* **Below:** *An eastern ribbon snake,* Thamnophis sauritus.

Dendrelaphis species, Tree Snakes

Dinodon species, Large-fanged Snakes

Drymobius species, Tropical Racers

Gonyosoma (syn. *Elaphe*) *oxycephala*, Arrow-headed Snake

Heterodon species, Hognosed Snakes

Leptophis species, Mexican Tree Snakes

Pituophis species, Pine or Bull Snakes

Thrasops jacksonii, Black Tree Snake

Subfamily Boiginae**, Rear-fanged Snakes

Ahaetulla nasuta, Green Tree Snake

Boiga species*, Mangrove Snakes

Chrysopelea ornata*, Flying Snake

Dispholidus typus**, Boomslang

Malpolon monspessulanus*, Lizard Snake

Oxybelis aeneus*, Vine Snake

Psammophis species*, Sand Snakes

Telescopus fallax*, Cat Snake

Thelotornis kirtlandii**, Twig Snake

Subfamily Dasypeltinae, Egg-eating Snakes

Dasypeltis scabra, African Egg-eating Snake

Subfamily Dipsadinae, Snail-eating Snakes

Dispas species, Snail-eating Snakes

Subfamily Homalopsinae, Aquatic Rear-fanged Snakes

Erpeton (syn. *Herpeton*) *tentaculatum**, Tentacled Snake

FAMILY ELAPIDAE**, Cobras and Coral Snakes

Bungarus species, Kraits

Dendroaspis species, Mambas

Micrurus species, Coral Snakes

Naja species, Cobras

Notechis species, Tiger Snakes

Pseudechis species, Black Snakes

FAMILY HYDROPHIIDAE**, Sea Snakes

FAMILY VIPERIDAE**, Vipers, Adders and Pit Vipers

Subfamily Viperinae, Vipers and Adders

Bitis species, Puffadders, Gaboon and Rhinoceros Viper

Cerastes species, Horned Viper

Echis species, Saw-scaled Viper

Vipera species, Adders

Subfamily Crotalinae, Pit Vipers

Agkistrodon species, Moccasins, Copperheads, etc.

Bothrops species, New World Pit Vipers

Crotalus species, Rattlesnakes

Lachesis species, Bushmaster

Sistrurus species, Pygmy Rattlesnakes

Trimeresurus species, Asiatic Pit Vipers

Index

Overleaf: 1) Pentastomid tongue worms, Armillifer armillatus, in the lung of Bitis gabonica. 2) Intestinal amoebiasis in Boa constrictor. 3) Secondary stomach inflammation in Morelia argus due to nematodes. 4) Pentastomid egg with fully developed larva, showing the rudimentary legs with claws. 5) Trematode eggs from ureter of Boa constrictor; the lids and larvae clearly visible. 6) Eggs of a primitive tapeworm of the family Pseudophyllidae in different developmental stages, from the feces of Elaphe radiata. 7) "Egg bundle" of a tapeworm in a protective shell, taken from the feces of Chondropython viridis. 8) Egg of tapeworm, Ophiotaenia sp., from Natrix natrix. 9) Egg of hairworm, Capillaria, a nematode. 10) Egg of the nematode Ophidascaris sp. from Bitis gabonica, showing the strongly sculptured shell. 11) Thin-shelled eggs of the nematode Kalicephalus sp. in different stages of development, taken from Elaphe longissima. 12) Free nematode larvae and eggs with embryos, genus Rhabdias, taken from lung mucus of Elaphe longissima.

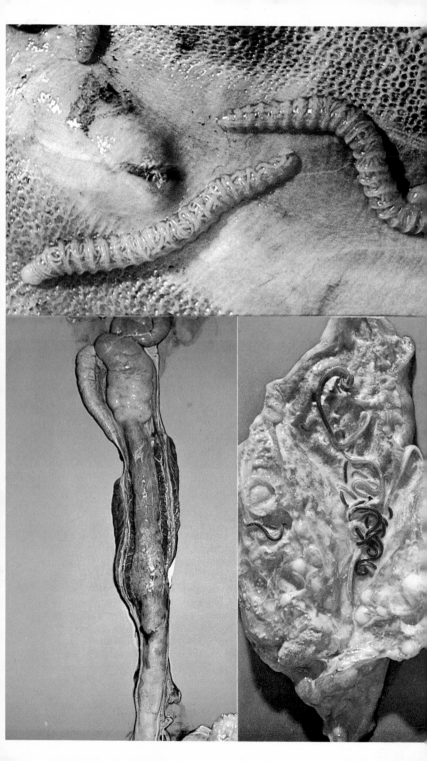

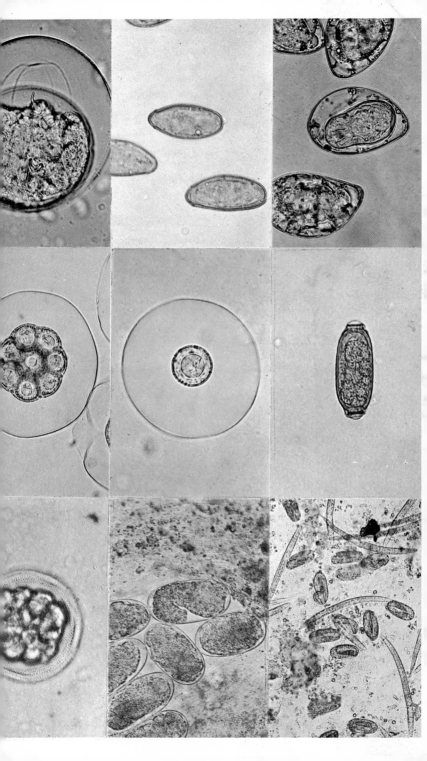

BOAS AND OTHER NON-VENOMOUS SNAKES
KW-002